Not So Common Sense

A Little Book of Reminders
for Those in Early Recovery

by

Mark A. Husk MA, LPC

PublishAmerica
Baltimore

First printing

PublishAmerica has allowed this work to remain exactly as the author intended, verbatim, without editorial input.

Softcover 978-1-4489-5091-1
PAperback 978-1-4512-4412-0
PUBLISHED BY PUBLISHAMERICA, LLLP
www.publishamerica.com
Baltimore

Printed in the United States of America

For Hallie

My Hope, My Joy
My Love, My Wife

Acknowledgments

This book is not a work solely of my own creation. It could have not been possible without the input and advise of numerous friends and family, and of course the many hours of conversations I have had with alcoholics and addicts from whom I have learned so much.

Introduction

"Common sense" is a rather over-used term. It seems however that many things that should be "common sense" usually isn't found to be so common. This is where the title of this book comes from. The ideas and insights in this book are not complex or difficult to understand. It takes no certain amount of education or background in psychological theory to understand these simple concepts.

Many of these aphorisms may appear to the lay reader to be "common sense", and not really worth the trouble of rehashing in a book about recovery. However, when people are in crisis, trying to heal their lives from years of abuse and neglect, trying to sort out the train wreck that they have woke up to find, thinking clearly is usually not one of their stronger points. Sometimes it takes an outsider looking in to point out the obvious, things that they have been blinded to because of everything else they have had to deal with. That's where I come in.

Recovering alcoholics and drug addicts have a huge uphill climb. Along with giving up their drug or drugs of choice, they may also be facing a wide variety of issues including legal problems, health problems, relationship problems, unemployment and everything else that can come along when an addict finally decides to get sober. With all these things to worry about, it's no accident that one of the mantras found in AA and NA rooms around the world is "Keep It Simple."

In over 18 years of working with alcoholics and addicts, I have found that keeping things simple has helped many people new to recovery stay sober. In my job as counselor, telling an addict how to work a recovery program is no good unless it can be broken down into more simple terms.

Just as we can recall lessons from simple aphorisms such as "Don't throw the baby out with the bathwater", and "Don't count your chickens before they're hatched", when we are dealing with something as complex and overwhelming as an addiction, axioms such as these can come in handy.

Many of the axioms in this book have come from my own conversations with addicts in early recovery. From the mouths of babes at times comes great wisdom. "You just gotta have the 'want to's'", a former client of mine used to say. Another was known to admit that "My addiction's name is Hank. Hank's trying to kill me." Or as another recovering addict used to say, "If I use, I break out in felonies."

Other sayings have come from my own attempts at trying to explain recovery principles to clients in early recovery, and needing to break down what I was saying into simple phrases that they could recall readily and use. Sometimes these sayings even became a mantra that I would use for myself. Things that I would tell my clients, "Sorry, the batteries in my Magic Wand are dead.", reminded me of my own limitations and boundaries.

This book was written with the addict in early recovery in mind. However, this book will also be useful for anyone dealing with an addict in their lives, including therapists, physicians, and family members. It provides common sense recovery reminders, as well as education about the nature of addiction and recovery. I hope you, the reader, will not let this book sit on a bookshelf, but take what you need and pass it on to someone else who may need to hear what it has to say.

1. You Gotta Do What You Gotta Do to Get to Where You Want to Be.

It's really easy to get lazy. We will do almost anything to make our lives easier.

Although there's nothing wrong with that, it can be a problem with us addicts. Trouble begins when we start avoiding our duties, cutting corners, and wasting time. For most people, these little things may be harmless. As people in recovery however, we need to remember that our sobriety depends strongly on our daily actions, great and small.

Working a recovery program doesn't just include going to meetings, calling our sponsor, or reading recovery literature. It also depends on us doing the best we can at whatever we do. We make this effort simply because that's just what we didn't do as active users. If we want to stay sober, then we need to act in the exact opposite ways we used to act when we were using.

But old habits die hard sometimes. We may find it tempting to cut out early from work, not do a job quite as carefully or as completely as we should, or let the dishes or laundry pile up, simply because we don't feel like putting forth the extra effort at the time. Our thinking errors can then start to surface, and we begin to rationalize and minimize our behavior. Next, we will begin to slip back into our old ways of dodging our responsibilities and avoiding our commitments. That's going to lead us to bigger trouble. Just as diligence keeps us sober, laziness can lead us right back to using, with the usual predictable results.

2. I'm Allergic to Alcohol.
If I Drink, I Break Out in Felonies.

When we first get clean, we are warned to stay away from all mood-altering drugs, alcohol included. If our drug of choice was not alcohol, then it may be hard for us to think that it's as harmful to us as other drugs we've used. We know that many people can drink normally without any consequences at all. They have a glass of wine with dinner, a beer or two after work, or on the weekend, all without loss of control. We might think that we should be able to do this, too. However, it's important to realize that as addicts, we are different.

By either practice or design, we are prone to abuse all mood-altering substances, which includes alcohol. There is something in us now that will always want to chase that high, to avoid uncomfortable feelings, or to reward ourselves by using a chemical. As a mood-altering drug, alcohol can do it for us. It also takes away our fine tuned judgment and increases our impulsiveness. That's just what makes it dangerous. And because it does these things for us, we can react to it just as we would any other mood-altering drug, by taking it to extremes.

3. Life—The Original.
Beware of Cheap Substitutes.

When we stop using and start going to meetings, we are warned to stay away from all "mood-altering substances". That's because we addicts have a nasty habit of getting out of control around any and all mood altering drugs, no matter what they are. It makes no difference what we are taking, or why we are taking it. It may be sleep aids, cough medicine, or even a prescription for pain, but if it alters our mood, we can abuse it.

The problem isn't just in the substance however. It's in the words "mood altering". As addicts, we love to have something that will make us feel better, to help us escape, or help us function a bit better. This is where other addictions besides drugs and alcohol can surface. Because we addicts have a bad habit of wanting to alter our moods, we can and will do almost anything to do it. It could be food, gambling, sex, work, exercise, or whatever else we find that does the trick. Anything we can take to extremes can help us numb out our emotions and replace facing real life with a cheap substitute.

So if we quit smoking pot and start working twelve-hour days, seven days a week, we're just exchanging one drug for another. By focusing on working so much, we don't have to deal with the problems that sobriety can throw at us. If we break a food addiction only to spend all day on the Internet, we're doing the same. Again, we find something that numbs us out, interferes with our life, and consequently, the lives of those around us, and nothing really changes.

4. You Can't Stand Around Mud Puddles and Not Expect to Get Splashed.

When we got sober, we knew there were some things we had to change. What usually came to mind was "the wrong crowd". We had to get rid of all of the people around us that used. Sometimes it's easy, other times it's not so easy. When it's easy, it's usually the people we didn't have much else in common with besides using. They were our friends as long as we had something, or could get something for them. Those kinds of people usually go away by themselves if we break off contact, simply because they can't use us anymore.

There are others though, who are a bit more difficult. They are our neighbors, relatives, old fishing/hunting buddies, people we have something in common with besides the drugs. The only problem with them now is that they still use. "It's ok", we may tell ourselves, "They know I don't use anymore and they don't use it around me. They don't even ask me to use."

That's all fine and good. But the real problem is not in how others treat us, but in how we treat ourselves. Remember that an addiction is not just a physical disease, it's a spiritual one as well. Just as our continued using changed us physically, mentally, and spiritually, getting sober does the same, except in reverse. It changes us so much that in time we begin to see subtle differences between ourselves and those around us that even casually use. We work to improve our thinking, our decision making and judgment, and we try to do what is best for us and our sobriety on a daily basis. We are developing new boundaries of what is right for us and what is not right for us, and as we grow along these lines, we will find that some of the beliefs and ways of thinking of those that use are not good for us anymore.

Even casual users can place a great value on their drugs and their lifestyle, and along with the using, comes the subtle, but harmful thinking and behavior that we are trying to change in ourselves. This type of environment we don't need in our lives, especially when we are new to recovery. The last thing we need to do is to get caught up in old thinking and behaving, and hanging around casual users is a good way to get there.

5. Working a Recovery Program Is Like Running Uphill in the Mud. If We Stop Running, We'll Slide Backwards.

We may have heard some people say, "I used to be an addict", or "I've recovered from alcoholism". It's as if they used to have a problem, and now it's over with and they have put it behind them. They seem to treat recovery as an event, as if they just got their car fixed. These people may have had a period in their life where they used a great deal, and then they just seemed to quit, without hospitals, without jails, and without the difficulty that we addicts go through in early recovery. It may however, be dangerous for us to think we can do the same.

Usually when people quit without much difficulty, it means that they probably don't have to change much else in their lives. It gives them license to keep on acting the same way they've been acting, and doing the same things they've always done. This for us, however, is asking for trouble. Sobriety demands constant improvement physically, mentally, and spiritually. And as a physical, mental, and spiritual disease, addiction stays with us for life. That in itself demands rigorous attention to where we are at in our recovery.

People with high blood pressure or diabetes must actively monitor themselves and their disease. They become experts on it, and can tell you intimately about the symptoms and latest progress in treatment. They know how the disease affects them, what limits they need to place on themselves, and how they need to treat themselves in order to stay healthy.

Dealing with the disease of addiction should be no different. Making constant adjustments in our sobriety, learning about new relapse prevention skills, talking with others who are also in recovery and learning how they stay sober, all of it is progress that is necessary to the recovering addict. Also just as important is making constant improvements in our own personal lives. We work on rebuilding the relationships with out spouses and children. We work on reducing our financial problems, and work to improve our education, job, living conditions, and such. This is important because it's about caring for ourselves. The more we work to make improvements in our lives, the more we can eliminate stressors and problems that lead to relapse. If we fail to continue to make changes for the better, then the same problems and situations will continue to arise, and we will continue to deal with them like we always have.

6. Beginning Recovery Is Like a Car Wreck in the Fog.

Every now and then we will see on the news where a pileup occurred on an interstate somewhere involving several cars. The reporter will usually attribute it to low visibility, or bad weather, and that many of the cars involved couldn't get stopped in time to avoid hitting the ones in front of them, causing a chain reaction pileup.

When we finally sober up, we often end up with more than our fair share of trouble. Not only are we now dealing with not using, we are also watching our past come back to haunt us with devastating force. Legal situations, money problems, and relationship problems suddenly pile up on top of us like a bunch of cars in the fog.

Now is the time we need the most support. We need to check our ego at the door and not try to get through this time alone. There is nothing wrong with asking for help at this point, and fortunately for us, help is everywhere. We can call up our family doctor for help with health problems, and a lawyer for legal problems. We can enlist the help of a psychologist, psychiatrist, or counselor familiar with addictions to help us with depression, anxiety, and other emotional problems. We can get a financial adviser to help us sort out our money problems, and a rabbi, priest, minister, or other spiritual leader to help us connect with a higher power. Most important of all, we need to get a sponsor to help us maintain our sobriety, and as many trusted family members and friends as we can. Also, we shouldn't overlook other sources of help such as free crisis counseling, the local food pantry, Salvation Army, and mission, and the local library and the internet for tons of useful information. We've worked hard to build up this mess, and now it's going to take a team of people to sort it out.

7. Denial Is Like Trying to Fight an Oncoming Train.

We can't fight a train. Everyone knows that. But many of us have lived in denial, believing that our using wasn't harming anyone, and that we were "just fine", and would remain "just fine" if others would just leave us alone. Our friends and family could see the reality of it, but somehow we, in our hearts, thought that we were in control, and that we were OK. It's really an eye opener though, when we suddenly realized that we were standing on the tracks, trying to fist fight the Overland Express.

For many of us, that was too big of a reality check for us to handle. Our first reaction was to deny that the train was even there. "What train?", we would say. "I don't see a train. How can there possibly be a train coming through here?". We seemed to have no problems, and nobody was getting hurt, and anyone that suggested otherwise obviously didn't know what they were talking about.

We might even have gone so far as to admit that, yes, we may be standing on train tracks, but trains never come through here. One hasn't come through yet, and even if it does, we know we can handle it. Our behavior may be risky, we might admit, but so what? There are no problems, hasn't been any, and there isn't going to be any, because we are in control. We're different.

Even when we finally do see the train, we try to minimize it. "It's not really that big. It's only a little train.", we say. When our using starts to cause problems, we don't really need to quit. It isn't that big of a deal. All we need to do is just cut down our use a bit and the problems will go away. Things aren't really as bad as others think they are, and we still can handle it. We're still in control. We had proof, too. We still worked, brought home a paycheck, provided for our kids, and certainly weren't as bad as some others we could name, who have lost jobs, homes, and family, who were in jails and hospitals and institutions. For our own peace of mind, we needed to hold onto the delusion that we were still doing OK, that despite the warnings, we were still in control.

When the train finally did hit us, we got quite a shock. When reality finally sets in, it strikes us as incredible that someone like us could be so out of control, and didn't even know it. The train was coming, and we were warned, but it was the drugs and our ego that kept us playing on the tracks, believing that everything was all right, until it was too late.

8. Being on a Dry Drunk Is Like Playing in Traffic.

Technically, being on a dry drunk is when we are exhibiting all the attitudes and behaviors of a user, but for the time being, we are just not using.

Now, we all know what will happen when someone tries to play in traffic. They will stand in the middle of the road, dancing or goofing off, while cars and trucks go whizzing by, missing them by inches. The only problem with the person playing in traffic is that even though they know they are taking a chance of getting hit, they really think it won't happen to them. Eventually though, a car, or a bus, or a speeding cement truck will come along and POW! Predictable, isn't it?

Many of us continue to do the same thing when we stop using. We continue to go to bars, hang out with our old using buddies, stay in the same bad relationships, do the same risky things, and think and react in the same old ways, believing that if we just don't use, then we're OK. These risky behaviors can be easy to see in others, but they may be hard for us to see in ourselves.

It's helpful when we are new to recovery to ask others close to us, our spouses, our sponsor, and others that we trust, to point out signs that they see in us that may signal a pending relapse. If we have been playing in traffic, they will probably identify things like our attitude, the way we talk, the way we act, or the way we respond to stressful situations. They may describe us as angry, spiteful, withdrawn, anxious, or defensive.

When those that love us gently (or not so gently) warn us of these signs, our job is to just shut up and listen, and to take into consideration that they may be right. We may be playing in the road and really not see the oncoming cement mixer with our name on it.

9. The Drug We're Using Ain't Got No Brakes.

When we are in recovery, especially after using some of the 'harder drugs', we may be tempted to think that other, more mild drugs may be safe for us. We might like to think that we may be able to go back to using recreational, or even some prescription drugs safely. We may think that because this 'milder' drug wasn't our drug of choice, or that a certain amount of time has passed, or that we plan to use it occasionally, or even if it is a drug prescribed by our doctor, it will be safe for us to use now.

However, we forget that the problem we have is not just with our drug of choice, but it's also a problem with ourselves. It's how we react physically, mentally, and spiritually to the use of a mood altering substance. If we've lost control over one (or more) mood altering substance, then the likelihood of it happening again with another drug is pretty good. Our addiction doesn't go away, and neither does our reaction to anything that alters our mood. This is why it's important to honestly examine our reasons for using any drug, prescribed or not, especially if we like to think of it as 'harmless'.

10. Don't Try to Fight a Fire by Yourself.

It's so heroic to try to get by with just our own wits and efforts. We take pride in being able to do things ourselves, to be able to say we don't need anyone's help. Yet, when it comes to taking on something obviously bigger than we are able to handle by ourselves, such as a house fire, we don't hesitate to call for help.

It's just the same in trying to stay sober. Although it's tempting to think that all we are doing is just not using anymore, we've got to remember that we are going up against a disease that is much more complex and deadly. We are trying to stay away from what used to be our best friend, what used to get us through the bad times (and not so bad times), and what used to comfort us and help us cope with the big bad world. Also, we need to consider that our addiction may not rest just in our behaviors, but in our very genetic makeup. There is strong evidence that the predisposition to addiction can be genetically transmitted from parent to child, just like heart disease and diabetes.

So, if we are fighting something that is so pervasive, so important, and so deadly as we know this addiction to be, it would be foolish to think that we wouldn't need anyone's help. Help comes in the form of meetings, sponsors, emergency phone numbers, recovery literature and having other recovering people around us. For us, battling a disease that we've seen ruin and kill people, trying to go it alone is not heroic, it's stupid.

11. We Gotta Protect What We Hurt.

Protecting an injury is a natural and instinctive action. If we hurt our hand for example, we would naturally want to take care of it and shield it from further injury. We might bandage it, hold it close to us, and take more care with it, lest we injure it again or make the injury worse through neglect. We know that if we ignore an injury and continue on as if nothing happened, the likelihood of the injury becoming worse increases. If it is an open wound, we stand the chance of it becoming infected. Left untreated, the infection could eventually kill us.

Whether we realize it or not, the same concept applies to our emotional wounds as well. Often we are told to just "let go and ignore" the cutting remarks of others. We are brought up to think that "words can never hurt us", and that we should just "forgive and forget" the hurtful things people say and do to us. So when we are emotionally wounded, we shrug it off, we ignore it, and stuff it, and pretend that nothing's wrong. And so our wound gets worse. It continues to eat at us, just like an infection, and eventually we are a walking emotional basket case just waiting for the opportunity to do something stupid.

When we are emotionally injured, when we are hurt, we have to take time out to heal. Fortunately, there is a way to do this. The first thing to do is to acknowledge the fact that we have been injured. We recognize the hurt and pain. We allow ourselves to feel angry, embarrassed, discounted, or shamed. The second thing we do is to remove ourselves from what it was or who it was that injured us. We need some space and time to sort things out and come to grips with these thoughts and feelings. Talking things out is always nice, but usually not a good idea when your emotions are high. The third thing we do is to actively seek out the support we need.

We call up good friends, we take a hot bath, we write out our thoughts and feelings in a journal, we go for a walk or a drive to sort things out. We take care of ourselves as much as we need to, and we defuse the emotional time bombs inside us. We do these things for ourselves, for our own serenity and peace of mind. We do these things for the person who injured us, so we may be able to address the issue in a calm and forthright manner. But most of all, we do these things for our sobriety.

12. Recovery from Addiction Is Like Changing Our Religion.

When we think of recovery, we think about the necessity of changing those people, places, and things that surrounded our using. However, what we may not realize is that a good and solid recovery is almost like changing our religious preference. This can be a very serious issue. It's not just changing churches, for example, going from a Baptist church and attending a Methodist church. It's more like an entire reconfiguration of our religious beliefs that would come from, for example, leaving Christianity and becoming a practicing Buddhist.

As an example, imagine ourselves belonging to a certain religious group. We may have been raised to believe that this group's views were correct and the only way to salvation. Our friends and families may belong to this group. We go regularly to this group's church, and participate actively in this group's practices and lifestyles.

Now if we come to the decision that this group may not have the answers we seek, or that what this group practices may not be right for us anymore, then we've got some major changes to go through.

First, we stop going to our former group's church. We stop hanging around other church members and quit the various church functions we were involved with. We lay down the law to our friends and relatives that we will not be part of this group anymore, nor can we afford for them to practice their religious beliefs around us, trying to influence our decision. We will get rid of our religious books, pamphlets, bumper stickers, jewelry, and other things that linked us to that group. We will strip away anything and everything that identifies ourselves as part of that group.

Now, if we decide to join another completely different religious group, we're gonna have to learn from scratch what it's all about. The best way

24

to learn is from members of that group. We may even find that many members of this new group joined for the same reasons that attract us. They too, may have become dissatisfied with their old religious beliefs and have sought out this group for solutions. As we listen and talk with them, we begin to learn who they are and what they believe. We ask questions about things we don't understand. We find out how they pray and what they hold sacred.

We listen to their sermons and read their books and literature with an open mind. We even learn what they do for fun. We hang out with them and participate in their social functions, and eventually, we become one of them. The things that we saw that drew us to that group we can now claim for ourselves, and we can use that knowledge to assist others coming behind us.

Recovery from addiction is no different. We see that what we are doing is not working, we decide to move in another direction, we get rid of all the garbage that came with our using, we seek out those who are sober and are in recovery, attend meetings, read recovery literature, and get a sponsor to help us work the steps. In doing so, we change our behaviors, our way of thinking, and literally our entire belief system, one step at a time.

13. A Loss Is a Loss Is a Loss.

It doesn't matter what we have in our lives, if we've got an emotional attachment to it, and we lose it, we miss it. We will miss it even if what we have lost wasn't good for us. And anything we miss, we're going to grieve its loss.

When we enter recovery, we are often reminded by those that care for us how bad those drugs were. Our own experiences can tell us that. But on the other hand, we can't deny that they did provide for us a great deal. They were our friends, our lovers, and our security blankets. Sometimes, our drugs meant more to us than life itself.

There is a grieving process everyone goes through when experiencing a loss. Although every experience differs in intensity and degree, it's a universal process. Aside from the stages of grief that we may have read about, there are also four basic tasks that we need to accomplish. We need to accept the reality of the loss, to experience the pain of the loss, to adjust to the new environment, and to reinvest ourselves in the new reality.

Sometimes it's hard to realize that when we put away our drugs, we can grieve its loss. To accept the reality of the loss, we realize that our drug is gone forever. There is no more casual use on weekends, holidays, or special occasions. It's gone from our lives forever.

It's almost second nature for us addicts to want to escape unpleasant feelings. However, once we let go and allow ourselves to experience the pain of the loss, only then can we begin to heal. Sometimes, the only way out of the pain is through the pain.

When we adjust to the new environment, we learn to live without our drugs. We begin to forge a new life with new interests and new friends. We also learn to handle stress, anger, fear, and learn to deal with all the frustrating situations that come with daily living without using.

When we reinvest in our new reality, we begin to live life comfortably. We set goals and achieve them. We have meaningful relationships and careers. We begin to honestly hold our head up high, because we finally have hope for our future.

Grieving is a healing process and naturally takes time. Each person works at it at his or her own pace. We put away and lay permanently to rest something that meant a great deal to us, in order to put into it's place something much more valuable and beautiful—life itself.

14. The More Tools We Have, the More Things We Can Fix.

When we first start going to meetings, those who have been in recovery for a while give us a lot of tools to use. They give us phone numbers to call, pamphlets and books to read, meetings to attend, people to talk to, steps to work, and slogans to memorize. If we come from a rehab or a treatment program, then we are given a lot of other things to do. We are given journals to write in, inventory forms to fill out, diets to follow, and even exercises to do. We may have even been given medicines to take, or been told to see a counselor or psychiatrist.

Do we really need to do these things? Our pride and ego, which we may have been listening to for quite a long time, will say, "No, of course not. I'm not weak, crazy, or powerless. All those things may be nice for others, but not for me. I can take it from here, thank you.". So we set our tools aside and try to continue on, just as we have been, without making any changes in how we deal with things.

What we tend to forget is, that life loves throwing us curve balls, especially just when we are not ready for them. The challenge comes when we try to deal with all these little surprises effectively, and without using. Without our tools, it's a lot easier for us to become over anxious, depressed, stressed out, and easier for us to make those mistakes we can't afford.

It's times like this when we need to reach for our toolbox. Just like a good mechanic will use his tools to keep his car in good condition, we need to use our own tools to keep us in good running condition. These tools are not there to completely solve our problems, but they make our problems a lot more manageable. When we go to meetings, watch our diet, do some journaling, or take time to call someone, we find that our worry, anxiety, and depression seems a little less overwhelming, and our problems a little easier to manage. Sometimes, that's just what we need to get through the day without using.

15. We Find Out Who Our Friends Are When We Go Broke, Go to Jail, Go to the Hospital, or Get Sober.

Anyone who has experienced any one of these knows that this is true. When we are in our greatest need, for company, for support, for encouragement, it's our true friends who always come through for us. Those others, who we may have thought were our friends, hang around us only until we are not useful to them anymore. When they are asked to give a little bit of their time or effort for us, they have a tendency to disappear, regardless of what we may have done for them. It's been said that a person is judged not by what they say, but rather by what they do. In this case, it's by what they don't do.

True friends however, are there when we need them. They give us rides to a doctors appointment or to a meeting. They will listen when we need to talk, even if it's 3:00 AM. They will visit us or write to us when we are in jail or the hospital. They will refrain from judging us too harshly, or be too critical or condemning of our actions. These are some of the markers of true friends.

If we are lucky enough to have these people in our lives, our job is to show our appreciation to them, and do what we can to keep them around us. We can show our gratitude by our actions, as well as our words. We can apologize and make amends to them for the harm we have done. We can tell these people just how much they mean to us, and specifically what we are thankful for. If they are ever in need, we can make sure that we are there for them, just as they have been for us. We continue to show our appreciation and support because, as we already know, they're kind of rare, and worth their weight in gold.

16. Reality Is the Interpretation of Facts.

When it comes to dealing with addiction, our mind is our greatest weapon. Unfortunately, it can also be our greatest enemy. Whether our mind is helping us or hindering us depends largely on what it is dwelling on. Although we like to think that we are usually in control over what we think and how we act, we can easily be affected by the very environment we are in.

Most of us have been frightened while watching a scary movie, or cheered on our favorite team on TV. What we are doing at that moment, is actually being influenced by an illusion. We are reacting emotionally and physically to an image projected onto a TV or a movie screen, and it has absolutely nothing to do with our own reality.

We can fool ourselves like this in other ways, too. If we surround ourselves with negative people who are always grumbling and complaining, we tend to get caught up in their talk and behavior, and start acting just like them. If we live in a chaotic environment with lots of noise and unpredictable stressful situations, we tend to react to that as well, and those stressors become part of us.

The same thing happens if we hang around those who drink and use. Their ways of thinking, talking, and acting rubs off on us, and we start to become one of them, even if we are not using.

As recovering people, we need to treat ourselves with care, especially when it comes to who and what we are exposed to. We begin to look at our surroundings with the idea that what surrounds us can affect us. It's our job now to reduce those negative influences, before they reduce us.

17. I'm Here Because I'm Crazy, Not Because I'm Stupid.

Addiction is no respecter of intelligence. It's no respecter of reason, or even common sense. It doesn't care who we are, or what kind of degree we have, or what we do for a living. It pays no attention to a person's IQ, wealth or social status. Go to any Alcoholics Anonymous or Narcotics Anonymous meeting. Here you will find doctors, lawyers, college professors, people who through their education and ability may have become leaders of the community. Yet, in listening to their stories, we will also hear tales of horror and madness and all of the out-of-control behavior expected from drunks and drug fiends.

It doesn't make sense, to those who haven't been there. How could a person of such high standing stoop to such levels? Surely, some ask, shouldn't these people know better than to do some of the things they talk about?

Of course we should know better. However, if we do know better than to do something, and we do it regardless, then that shows that we have lost our ability to think rationally. It means that there is something else that is driving our decisions and actions rather than our knowledge, experience, or wisdom. This is the very definition of insanity. And that thing that has taken control over us is of course, addiction.

Addiction doesn't care much about us, or about others. It will lie, cheat, steal, even kill to get what it wants. It will eat us alive, forcing us to do anything and everything it wants, just to get another hit. It will destroy our jobs, our friends, our loved ones. It will take away our health, our wealth, our freedom, and our lives.

The worst part about this insanity is that addiction never learns it's lesson. It's been proven time and again that the consequences we face don't matter much. We can lose everything important to us and still continue to use. We can even get everything back just to lose it all over again. Time spent away from using doesn't matter much either. We can be sober half a lifetime and our addiction can still come back, just as deadly as before. As long as we are alive, it will be with us, tugging at us, whispering in our ear, just so it can get what it wants.

The founders of AA knew this very well from our own experiences. The Second Step of AA talks about restoring us to sanity. It stood to reason that, if we were so powerless over this illness, then something or someone would have to restore our sanity for us. This would, by necessity, have to be a Power greater than ourselves. Many of us have found that Power in the groups and programs of AA and NA. It has helped us restore our sanity, and become once again respectable people.

So now, when we are telling our stories to others who may wonder how someone like ourselves could have done the things we did, we can simply tell them, "I'm here because I'm crazy, not because I'm stupid".

18. Welcome to the Human Race.

It's easy to kick someone when they're down. Especially if it's ourselves we are kicking. When it comes to beating ourselves up, nobody does it better than we do. And we can find all kinds of reasons to beat ourselves up. It can be for something we did or didn't do in the past, or our failure to live up to our own expectations now. We kick ourselves by our constant negative self talk, reminding ourselves over and over again that we are stupid, failures, and general good-for-nothings.

It seems funny that when we were using, we used to pile the blame for all our failures and disappointments on everyone and everything else but ourselves. It was our job, our spouses, the money situation, anything but us. None that we are sober, sometimes we can't seem to take enough of the blame. The very things that we would readily forgive anyone else for without even a second thought, we torture ourselves for over and over again. Having some feelings of guilt about our wrongdoing is healthy. It spurs us on to make amends, to take action and undo some of the damage we have done. However, when we wallow in our guilt and shame so much that we are constantly in misery, all we do is continue to hurt ourselves needlessly. We are also probably making everyone else around us miserable as well.

There are certain steps we can take to make this better. The most obvious is of course the making of amends. We also remind ourselves of the slogans we see at every AA and NA meeting: "Let Go and Let God", "Take It Easy", "Live and Let Live", "Just For Today", and "Keep It Simple". We also listen to the stories of those who have gone before us, who have developed the serenity we are looking for. As we take these steps, we learn to forgive ourselves, as well as others. We come to realize that it's OK to allow ourselves, and those around us, to be fallible, to be in the wrong, and to make mistakes. Taking on this bit of humility doesn't, as we might expect, make us appear to be weak or soft, but as we soon learn, serves to make us stronger, by showing us what it truly means to be human.

19. Sometimes You Just
Gotta Stop and Ask for Directions.

We all get lost sometimes. We take a wrong turn, or miss an exit, and suddenly we find ourselves in unfamiliar territory. As feelings of confusion, bewilderment, or even panic starts to rise within us, we know that there are several things we can do. We start to look around for clues, road signs, or landmarks to tell us where we are. We may get out the road map and puzzle over it. Or we may just keep driving around until we get back on the right path. These actions are often effective in getting us out of small jams. But when we are really lost, stuck out in the middle of nowhere, they may be of little or no help to us at all.

That's when we have to swallow our pride and ask for directions. And usually, with a few kind words from a stranger, we are off on our way again, a little less confused and a bit more relieved. For many of us, asking someone for directions may be an easy task, something we do as a matter of course. For some of us however, the mere thought of asking for help makes us cringe. To us asking for help is a sign of weakness, of our inability to do things for ourselves. We shudder to even think of needing to ask someone for assistance.

However, even as strong and as capable as we may be, it's very common in recovery to run into situations that are a bit bigger than we are capable of handling by ourselves. When we start to feel overwhelmed, when our feelings of anger or frustration become too great, when we start overreacting, or just not caring anymore, then it's time for us to stop and ask for directions.

Of course in these situations, a stranger along side the road may not be our best resource. The best directions for us will come from those who have not only been there and knows the way back, but also knows us as well. So we call our sponsor, or counselor, our family, or our best friends. They know just what we need to hear, and what we need to do, to get us back on the right road.

20. If Our House Is on Fire, We Don't Stop to Pack Our Bags Before We Get Out.

How do we know we're in trouble? What kind of warning signs do we look for? Are there areas of our lives that present certain dangers to our recovery?

Each of us has our own individual weaknesses and slippery areas. There are some warning signs of relapse however, that apply to all of us. When we see these, it should be like a smoke alarm going off in our house.

One of these areas that present warning signs is the use of our recreation time. In its worst and most obvious case, we may find ourselves visiting old haunts. We start to frequent the local corners where we used to hang out, the bars, the old using friends. These are obvious danger areas to be certain. When we find ourselves in these places, anyone could see that we are flirting with relapse. What is less obvious however, is the old "stinking thinking" that got us there. It may be for us the longing for the "good times" of the past. We might miss our old friends, things that are familiar to us, or simply want an escape from the stress of daily living. We may tell ourselves that we can just stop by to visit, just for a minute, and because we don't pick up, it's OK.

This type of thinking needs to be paid close attention to. When we see it in ourselves, we need to get to a meeting and get ourselves a reality check.

Another area is the management of our financial lives. Are the bills paid? Do we have our debt managed? Do we have a stable job? Do we even have food in the house? These are problems that we may have fought constantly in our using days. Now that we are sober, the continued mismanagement of our finances is another stressor that we just don't need.

Obviously, it's important to get our financial house in order when we are new to recovery, but later on down the road, we still can't afford to let ourselves get in caught in a financial bind. Part of our serenity comes from knowing that we are doing all we can to live within our means, pay our debts, and spend what we have left over wisely. Shut off notices and overdue bills may have been common in our past, but when we see them now, we need to realize that something is going wrong with our sobriety.

Our relationship with others is another major area. When our relationships are unstable, when we fight and argue constantly, when we live with suspicion, distrust and fear, they become an emotional battleground where there can be no winner. We find ourselves angry, resentful, jealous, obsessive, and controlling. None of this is good for our sobriety. Many of us have worked hard to get sober only to relapse again due to the crazy relationships that remained, but weren't addressed as important issues.

Even here, help is available if we are bold enough to reach out. Literature on relationships abound, and some of it is very good. Advise from those in recovery once again can prove invaluable. Often, we will find that many of those we find in AA or NA meetings have faced the same obstacles. Alanon was created specifically for those dealing with addicts in our lives. Marriage counseling is another, sometimes overlooked option. Sometimes our relationships can be fixed, sometimes they can't. The most important thing though, is to do whatever we can to keep our serenity and peace of mind.

Usually, it's not having the drug thrust in our face by well meaning using friends that gets us to relapse, but our failure to deal with our own thoughts and emotions, which are a direct result of the situations we are in. Our management of our free time, our money and our relationships are major areas, and can't be taken for granted or overlooked. If we remain aware of how we conduct ourselves in these areas, and take immediate action when things start to get out of hand, we won't find ourselves trapped with the proverbial house burning down around us, and find ourselves facing the consequences of another relapse.

21. It's Not My Job, Man.

We can only do so much. We can only give so much, and we can only take so much. We all have our limitations. Yet, we are a nation of martyrs and heroes. The belief that we should do for others at our own expense is deeply ingrained in us.

There is nothing wrong with wanting to do for others. It does become wrong however, when we ignore our own needs for their benefit. We may have seemingly endless demands and expectations from family, friends, neighbors, coworkers, and our boss. Add to this our inability or unwillingness to set limits on what we will do for others, then the damage done to ourselves can be horrendous. We stay in bad jobs or in abusive relationships. We put up with unbelievable chaos and stress. We get run over, pushed around, and used. What we get in return for our sacrifice is worry, anxiety, and despair. We get headaches, ulcers, lots of sleepless nights, and really, really tired.

In the twelve step programs, we are reminded to put "First Things First". This says we have to set some boundaries and priorities in our lives. There are some things we certainly need to do for others. There are some things we do for others simply because we enjoy doing them. Other things however, we may do because we feel that it's what we "should" do, or because we believe that either we or someone else would feel bad or hurt if we didn't. We may feel obligated and pressured, maybe even intimidated or threatened.

It's important that we make a clear distinction between these. Whenever we feel obligated, or pressured into doing something, we should take a good close look at what it also does to us. Other peoples' demands on our time and energy can have negative effects on our own lives, and can lead us right back into the chaos we know so well. It's times like these, when we are asked or expected to sacrifice our serenity or priorities for the ease and comfort of others when it's OK to say, "Sorry, I can't do that right now." We simply and firmly refuse and stick by it.

This is not an act of selfishness, as some might accuse, but an act of self-protection. We have our own limits and our priorities. It's our job to know what they are and to respect them. To violate these means to risk our own sanity and our sobriety. This does no one any good. But when we keep our priorities in line, and stay within our limits, we find then that we are not only taking care of ourselves, but we are actually taking better care of others around us as well. We have more time and energy, more peace of mind, and our sobriety as well. Not a bad tradeoff for not doing something.

22. Sorry, the Batteries in My Magic Wand Are Dead.

We can't fix people. We can't work miracles. There is only so much we can do.

Once we have been relieved of the pain of our addiction, it's only natural that we want to reach out to help others. Our enthusiasm to share our newfound answers is wonderful. However, as human beings dealing with other human beings, we have our limits. As much as we want to share what we have found, we can't expect others to jump at the life-ring we have thrown them. As much as we want to be part of their salvation from the pain and misery we can obviously see in them, we must remember that their recovery depends a great deal on their taking the first step. We can talk to them, visit them, call them, and drag them to meetings, but if they do not make any effort to help themselves, then our hands are tied.

Sometimes others who have seen a change in us, and realize that we now do not hesitate to help those in need, will expect us to run to the rescue of themselves or others that they direct us to. "So and so needs help, and I wonder if you would talk with them", they might say. And they might have great expectations of us, (or even we of ourselves), and then, if the person isn't "fixed", then we may seem to be at fault.

The truth is, we can't fix people. As much as we'd like to reach out and save those who are still suffering, we are limited as to what we can do. Other people, just like us, have their own choices to make. We made ours, for better and for worse, and have paid the consequences when we were wrong. Others have the right to do that, too. They have the right to refuse our help. We can however, make sure that when someone does finally get sick and tired of being sick and tired, and they do reach out for help, that our hand is there.

23. If God Has Bigger Plans for You, Then Don't Get in His Way.

In the Third Step of most, if not all, Twelve Step programs, it says, "Made a decision to turn our will and our lives over to the care of God as we understood Him.". For most of us, this is a very tall order. As active users we built up quite an ego. The entire world revolved around us. Many of us thought we were in control, that we had things worked out, that we were all right. Then Fate threw us that curveball.

When we finally got sober, our first instinct was to grab the reins and get back in the drivers seat, and back to controlling our own lives. Many of us thought that we could take charge and do things differently this time.

However, if we acknowledge that we are dealing with an addiction that is greater than ourselves, then it stands to reason that we may not be the best choice for running our own lives. That's when we need to seek out a Power greater than ourselves, and let it run the show. What this means, is that if there is a Power greater than ourselves directing our lives, then we should realize that at times our desires, plans, and goals may not be in accord with the direction that our Higher Power wants us to go.

Turning our will and our lives over to a Higher Power doesn't mean that we lose the ability to chose what we want for our own lives. What it means is that we check in with our Higher Power on a daily basis to make sure we are on the right track. We may pose questions, situations, and decisions and then listen to what it has to say.

Trusting in our Higher Power to know what is best for us can be difficult however, because in doing so, we need to give up a few things.

The first thing we need to give up is our over-inflated ego. We lose our sense of self importance that usually got us into arguments, caused resentments, and turned us into loners. What we get in return is true humility, the ability to rejoin the human race, and to laugh at ourselves for being fallibly imperfect.

The second is worry and fear. If there is Someone else at the helm of our lives, and that Someone is greater than us, then we should trust in that Someone to take care of us, and get us through the things that scare us. When we recognize our own limitations and turn things over to our Higher Power, then we can relax and enjoy the journey of our lives, no matter the circumstances.

The third is anger and frustration. Just as our Higher Power will take care of our future, we can let it take care of our present as well. Situations that we can't manage on our own without blowing our top we can turn over to our Higher Power. Our Higher Power should know how to handle our problems much better than we do. By turning them over, we can let go of the desire to control our situation and relax, trusting that everything is going to work out for the best.

Giving up these things isn't easy. We may have practiced them until they are second nature to us. But these are the very things that can keep us from the serenity and happiness that we seek. They stand in our way, and block the very path that our Higher Power has laid out for us.

24. There Are Two Kinds of People Who Will Never Understand What We Are Going Through; the Ones Who Have Never Been There, and the Ones Who Are Still There.

The ones who have never been there have no idea what it's like to go through the pain and struggles of addiction and recovery. They may be our friends, family members, or people we work with. These people have never had a problem with any mood-altering drug, or had to face the chaos and problems that addiction brings. They have no idea what it's like to lose control. They have never had cravings strong enough to make them sacrifice something dear to them, or continued to do something that they know is destroying their lives, despite consequences.

Due to this lack of experience, these people may have a difficult time understanding why we can't have just a glass of wine, or a beer with the guys, or go out to a bar on a Saturday night. They may question why we may need to leave a party, or go to a meeting, or call our sponsor.

It's times like these, when we've got to take care of ourselves and our addiction, that we do what's best for us, regardless of whether others understand our actions or not. Our addiction makes us a little different, and we have certain rules to follow, which don't apply to those who don't have this disease.

If we are fortunate, those close to us may sincerely want to understand us. They may ask questions, listen when we need to talk, maybe even attend meetings with us. But we can't expect them to completely understand our addiction, or our process of recovery. What we are going through may not make sense to them and despite their best intentions, they won't be able to help us when we need it.

On the other hand, there are those we may run into who are still actively using. From where they are, they can't see the consequences of our use. Their own active addiction has blinded them, just as it did us, to the fact that we are dealing with a progressive, chronic and fatal disease, something that willpower and self control has very little to do with. Needless to say, these active users are dangerous to our sobriety. We can't expect them to respect our abstinence, or even to understand our recovery, simply because they haven't taken that journey themselves.

25. If You Keep a Baby from Falling Down, It Will Never Learn to Walk.

We are taught from the time we are little to care for others and keep them from getting hurt. We are taught to be comforters, soothers, healers, and caretakers. Not a bad thing, really. However, when dealing with addiction, the caretakers of this world have to take what may seem to be an unusual stance. Sometimes, it's good for us addicts to feel the pain we have caused ourselves and others. When we needed to learn that we were powerless over a substance, it was usually the natural consequences of our actions that taught us that lesson. These lessons couldn't be learned as long as we were sheltered and protected by well meaning people. They had to go away, to stop bailing us out, in order for us to fully see the damage we were doing. By fully experiencing the consequences of our actions, by sometimes literally falling down, we finally get the message and began to learn to walk.

26. The Knife That Cuts Flesh Can Also Cut the Bread.

As human beings living around other human beings, we carry a great responsibility, to ourselves and to others. As recovering addicts, our responsibility intensifies ten fold. When we were using, we caused a lot of damage. It wasn't just the wrecked cars, broken furniture and so forth, but also the invisible damage we caused, including the unkind words, lies, and deceit to our spouses, family and friends.

In tallying up the damage, we should also include what may be called the "loss of potential". If we were sober all that time, and had our heads about us, what good might we have accomplished? What goals could we have achieved?

Now that we are finally sober, we owe it to others, and most importantly to ourselves, to make amends, to heal the wounds, and use our hands, head and heart to heal instead of hurt. We need to get in touch with that person inside us that would have lived life much differently, that perhaps would have made a difference in a more positive direction. We can never undo the past, but we can actively work toward improving ourselves, and our community where we live. To become actively involved in something that heals, comforts and supports others and ourselves is some of the best work we can do.

27. Drunk Stuff Happens.

When we finally sober up, guilt and shame tends to play a great part in our lives. Once our conscience comes back on line, we are reminded, either by our memory or perhaps by others, of what we have done. We look into the eyes of those we've hurt, and we feel all the pain from the damage we have done. How can we make up for all of this? Sometimes, the feelings of guilt and shame over our actions (or inactions) can readily drive us back to using.

How do we keep this from happening? When we take a closer look at our addiction, we realize that we weren't the only ones in control. We all know that addiction takes over our minds, but we sometimes forget that it also influences our decisions and actions. It dictates what we do, what we say, and who we hurt. It has no sense of ethics, no morals, no real sense of right or wrong except when it comes to protecting its own.

Sure, we are responsible for what we have done, but we weren't making these choices sober. We were using, and causing hurt and pain to those around us is what users do. It's a symptom of the disease we have and underlines our own loss of control. Had we been fully in control of ourselves, we wouldn't have done have the things we did. So, even though we should take responsibility for our actions, we need to realize that we were acting at the time as addicts, not as sober, rational people.

28. Babies Cry, Water Runs Downhill, and Jerks Are Gonna Be Jerks.

Some things are just a fact of nature. Babies cry, and water runs downhill. We all know this, and when it happens, we can accept it without much complaint. We don't get too upset over them. It can be the same with people. We all know people who are usually nice. They smile and act friendly, they greet us with a warm hello, and we feel good when we are around them.

Others however, tend to act just the opposite. They are mean, nasty, spiteful, inconsiderate and selfish. If we can avoid these people, it's best of course, that we do. Sometimes however, they are unavoidable, and we find ourselves upset and angry over their rude and offensive manners. It's times like these that it helps to remember that these "jerks" are really just another part of the entire fabric of life, and if we let ourselves react negatively to them, we are more likely to harm our own serenity than correct their behavior. So, if someone is acting in an ill manner towards us, we don't have to take it personally and get ourselves upset over their actions. If we can remember that these malcontents are just a small rotten spot on an otherwise beautiful world, then it tends to make them a little easier to deal with, and helps us preserve our sanity and our sobriety. We can deal with them in a more calm and accepting manner, without becoming a victim to their negative attitude or behavior.

29. There Are Two Times When Relapse Can Happen: When Things Are Going Bad, and When Things Are Going Good.

When we first get sober, there are many things we are told to do to help insure us against relapse. We are often told to identify and watch out for slippery areas. We are told to be aware of and avoid dangerous people, places, and things. We are told to pay attention to the acronym "HALT", and not let ourselves get too Hungry, Angry, Anxious, Lonely, or Tired.

When we think about the causes of relapse, we may think of bad situations, or stressful events that may drive us back to using. However, there is another side of relapse that we need to be aware of. Many of us relapse when things are going well for us. Just when we get our act together, our feet on the ground, and our lives settled, we seem to self destruct. To those around us, and even to ourselves, our relapse can be very puzzling. Why would we want to ruin our lives when things are finally going well for us?

What usually happens is that we drop our guard. Our old stinking thinking comes back, and we have lost our defenses against it. There may be several reasons behind this. A long time may have passed since our last use, and we have stayed sober successfully for so long, that we may think that we are out of danger. Many of our old problems may have vanished, and we are sailing on smooth waters. We may start to think that perhaps our using didn't really have a lot to do with the consequences we have worked so hard to overcome. We may get so caught up in our new life that we lose touch with the recovering community, and stop using our recovery tools. We may become involved with others who can casually use and not suffer the consequences that we have. In order to fit in, we may be tempted to try it also.

In all the good times, we can end up forgetting the consequences of our use. We lose our identity as a person recovering from a chronic, progressive, fatal disease. Our recovery loses it's importance in our lives, and from there, it's easy to go downhill.

30. Hank's Trying to Kill Me.

It's important when we get sober to realize that we are dealing with not just a mistake, or a problem that can be readily solved and forgotten, but with a chronic, deadly disease.

There was a fellow in the program that used to say, "I have an addiction. My addiction's name is Hank. Hank's trying to kill me." He saw his addiction as a relentless killer, bent on taking his life however it could. He would describe the different things that "Hank" would whisper to him. "Go ahead. You deserve a beer. It won't hurt you." He talked about the obstacles and temptations "Hank" put in his path, such as using situations and opportunities. He knew also, that "Hank" could use his emotions and even his friends, family, and the people around him as weapons, trying to get him to use again.

This type of thinking kept this fellow on his guard. He knew that Hank was sneaky, and was always looking for a different tactic, a different weapon to use against him. Today it might be a beer commercial on TV. Tomorrow it might be an unexpected bill, or running into an old using friend. This fellow knew that whatever it took, Hank was willing to go to any lengths to see him dead.

It was because of his ability to separate his own using thoughts and desires from himself that helped him recognize the dangers and keep him sober. He saw his addiction as a separate part of himself, one that wouldn't go away, but one that he could fight as well.

As much as Hank tried to kill him, our friend used every tool at his disposal to fight back. He attended regular meetings, had a sponsor, read recovery literature, and made use of the telephone. He concentrated strongly on keeping his sobriety, studying the steps and working the program. Whatever it took he would do, because he knew that if he dropped his guard, Hank would find a way to kill him.

31. You Just Gotta Have the "Want To's"

As we sit in AA and NA meetings, we will usually hear a tale of someone's relapse. They will tell how they were clean for several months or even years, and then went back to using. To those of us who are newly clean, or haven't relapsed, this can be puzzling at the least, even frightening. When we listen to their stories, several factors may be identified that may have interfered with their sobriety. They may have lost a loved one, they may have fallen on hard times, or they may have become depressed or ill. In any case, there is usually one thing that each person who has relapsed has in common. They lose their focus on their sobriety. Somehow, or someway, they forgot where they have been, and what they are staying sober for. They lost their sense of gratitude. They lost the "want to's".

So how do we keep this from happening? How do we ensure against relapse and a trip back down the same road we worked so hard to get off of? How do we keep that spark of gratitude alive in us?

There are several basic things we need to do that will help us keep relapse at bay. One thing is to develop and maintain a conscious contact with a Higher Power. This will help us by giving us a source of strength and hope when we need it most. It's also important to stay in contact with other recovering people. By going to meetings, by listening to other's stories, by telling our own, we are reminded of where we have come from, what happened, and what it is like now, for ourselves and others. We hear of their struggles, their victories, and their defeats, and we are reminded of ourselves. Also, as suggested in the Twelfth Step, we help other addicts stay clean. By being of service to others, we are shown face to face the struggle it takes to get sober and stay sober. In working with other addicts, we see ourselves in them. We also are reminded just how far we've come in our journey. By doing these things, by making them part of our daily lives, we develop and keep the "want to's" and ward off those compulsions and temptations that come with our disease.

32. Never Try to Swim While Carrying an Anchor.

When we first get sober, we are told to get rid of all the old people, places, and things that are associated with our using. Some of these are easy to identify. They are our using friends, our dealer and buyers, the local corner or bar where we used to hang out, or even our favorite store where we used to buy our alcohol.

However, there may be other things in our lives that could negatively affect our sobriety that isn't easily identifiable. These may include our non-using friends, our jobs, our neighborhood, even our significant others. These may cause us stress and problems that we don't need in our lives, especially when we are starting to learn to live sober.

If the people around us don't support our sobriety, if they are mean spirited, discontent with their lives, negative in their attitudes and behaviors, if they are argumentative and disagreeable, then they have little place in our lives. Just as we need to avoid the influences of those who actively use, we also need to avoid the influences of these people as well. Other people's misery is infectious, and we can catch it if we hang around them long enough.

Once we become sober, we may find out that we can no longer do the job we used to. The work we used to do intoxicated, we may find too difficult and stressful for us now that we don't have our drug of choice to lean on. Being newly sober can be stressful, and working at a difficult job or in a stressful environment may be too much for us. As recovering addicts, we realize that we have our limitations, and we must respect them. If our job or work environment demands more of us than we are capable of doing without using, then we need to evaluate whether it is really worth keeping. No job, whatever the pay, is worth our misery and our sobriety.

Many times we find that as active addicts, we ended up living in some pretty poor environments. Now that we are sober, we may need to rethink whether continuing to live there is healthy for us or not. We should be concerned not only with our safety, but with our sobriety and our serenity as well. In our old neighborhoods there may be those who we have made enemies with and wish us ill. There may be those old haunts, those corners, those places that we know are always available, should we decide to use again. Once again, our sobriety must come first, and although in the past we may have moved to try to get sober, now we may need to move in order to stay sober.

As active users, we may have put our significant others through hell. We may finally sober up to find that perhaps irreparable damage has been done to the relationship. Although many recovering addicts make amends and regain their relationships with their family and friends, some do not. In these instances, trust is lost, respect is lost, honesty is lost, and the commitment to the relationship itself is nonexistent. Because a relationship with another person requires work from both, if one is not able or willing to do their share, then the relationship cannot work. The result is more stress, pressure and emotional pain that could easily jeopardize our recovery.

33. There's a Lot More to Being Sober Than Just Being Sober.

When we finally sober up, and the drugs are out of our system, we can get on what is called a "pink cloud". The world is wonderful. We feel great. We are on an almost constant natural high. We may begin to think that we have this sobriety thing licked.

What is difficult to see, especially at this time, is that our work is not done. In order to stay sober, we still have some work to do. That "pink cloud" will fade with time, and one day things won't look so cheerful. The reality of having to live life on life's terms will set in, and those old feelings that we used to cover up with drugs will come back. We become angry, anxious, lonely, bored, and depressed. If we don't do something at this point, we are in trouble. There are however, several things we can do, if we are willing to do them.

One of these is to use a telephone. When we started going to meetings, other recovering addicts gave us their phone numbers. These people weren't doing this just to be nice. When they gave us their phone numbers, they were saying to us that they knew where we have been. They knew the loneliness of the newly recovering person. They sincerely wanted to help keep us sober. When we start to feel those old rotten nagging feelings rising again, it's time to put those phone numbers to use. Sometimes, just to hear a friendly voice that understands, and one that can tell us with confidence that things are going to get better, can make all the difference in the world.

Another action we can take is to go to meetings. When we have a problem, situation, or question about our sobriety, the best place to find an answer is among a group of people who specialize in it. Here we can hear others who have been down the same road we are on, sharing their experiences, their strength, and their hope. It's likely that in a meeting there is someone who will have just the answer we need.

We can also read the recovery literature. In addition to the AA Big Book, and the Basic Text of NA, other literature from daily meditations, personal stories of recovery, and quick and ready advice for recovery oriented problems can be found in any bookstore. The spiritual orientation of much of the recovery literature can put us back in touch with our Higher Power, and give us gentle reminders of the truly important things in our lives.

The use of a good sponsor can be invaluable. From being there when we need them, to helping us work the steps, they get to know us inside and out. They can often see through our little cover-ups, and confront us when we really need it. They know when something is not right with us, and can gently badger us till we fess up. They help keep us honest, and give us the motivation and inspiration to keep going.

We can also work the steps. When we start attending meetings, we may hear others talk of working the steps. These twelve steps are the actions suggested by those who have traveled down the same path we are on now. It is a program of action that works for them, and helps keep them sober. It takes a lot of thought, some writing, some working with others, and quite a bit of doing things we'd probably just as well not do. It helps us confront our fears, make amends, and find strength and hope along the way. As a program of personal transformation, it's not the easiest, but it's free, and for many, it works.

This is just the start of a lifelong journey of self exploration and improvement. As we work our program, and use the tools that are available to us, our confidence, joy, and serenity grows.

34. You Gotta Build the Foundation Before You Put the Roof On.

When you build a house, you have to have a strong foundation. Many things in a house can be adjusted, changed, or repaired, but the foundation is one thing that, if it is weak, is something you are stuck with. A weak foundation can ruin a perfectly good house. Although a house may look fine from the outside, if the foundation is weak, it will soon began to crack and crumble, and eventually will be worthless and beyond repair.

When we are new to recovery, we are often told to take it easy, to not complicate our lives, and to get the basics of sobriety down. We are also told to behave in ways that may seem restrictive and unnecessary to us. We are told to stay away from any mood altering chemical, to go to several meetings a week, stay away from using friends, change our diet, change the people, places, and things in our lives, and so forth.

Many of these things we wonder about, for they may seem harmless to us, and we see others who may have years of recovery doing the things we are told not to do. It doesn't seem like a recovery program to us, one that will allow us to live our lives comfortably without using. But just as you can't tell much about a house from looking at the foundation, you can't see what your recovery will look like later down the road.

Like most people, we want results, and we want them now. Patience is usually not one of our strong points. However, if we listen to those in long term recovery, they will tell us to slow down, take it easy, relax a bit, and not expect things so fast. Results will come, but only after we pay close attention to the basics. Changes in our lives will come, and we will get the serenity we are seeking. Many of the rough areas of our lives will get better, but only if we take the time to work things out slowly and carefully, one day at a time. We spent a long time learning to use, and we learned it well. Now we need to take time to learn to be sober. And that starts with laying a good foundation.

35. There Ain't No Easy Way Out.

There is nothing wrong with wanting to escape emotional or physical pain. The desire to get away from something that is hurting us is a natural instinct, and when it works the way it's supposed to, it helps keep us healthy, safe, and alive.

As addicts however, we tend to take even this to extremes. When we were using, it was common for us to use to escape the emotional pain of one thing or another. Whether it was a bad job, bad relationship, or anything else that caused us discomfort, the way around it was simply to change the way we were feeling, which we could readily do with the help of the right chemicals.

Now that we are sober, our chemical coping mechanism is gone. Left to us is the stark bright light of reality. Where we used to hide and numb ourselves out with our chemicals, we now have to face reality without our crutch. It's something we're not used to not having with us. Also, in addition to facing the regular, normal levels of anxiety and depression we all face, we are asked to address all the damage we have done, our legal problems, health problems, relationship issues, and do it without our security blanket. It's enough to make anyone want to run and hide.

The only problem is that we can't run and hide. As much as we want to, we can't take the easy way out. Although we may feel ashamed, afraid, embarrassed and so forth, our sobriety depends on our facing these problems and dealing with them.

Fortunately, we don't have to do this alone. Here's where the advise, support, and guidance from our recovering friends comes into action. They have been where we have been, and have walked through the same fire we are now going through. They know how to handle these problems, and how to do it sober. They can give us advise, contacts, and a sympathetic ear. They can also give us directions on how to face the problems we have. There may not be an easy way out of the mess our addiction has created, but there is a way out, and we don't have to go it alone.

36. You Can Only Put So Much Air into a Balloon.

Balloons are wonderful things. They go from some small limp piece of rubber to a large colorful round symbol of merriment and joy. But when we blow up a balloon, we have to pay attention as to how much air we put in. It's just when a balloon is big and full is when it's also at it's most fragile. Just a puff or two more of air, and BANG!, the thing blows up in your face. There is a fine line between having a balloon that is just right and one that is ready to burst.

In many ways, we are like these balloons. We get under pressure by the people, places, and things we have let into our lives. Some are unavoidable, but some aren't. When our balloon bursts, the explosion can be severe, especially with us addicts. We may relapse and return to using, starting up again the same old nightmare of pain and chaos that we worked so hard to escape from. More commonly however, we react just like most others do. We bite the head off of those closest to us. We become irritable, grouchy, bitchy, and just a pain in the butt to live with. We may explode and yell over little slights and problems, over reacting enough to send those around us running for cover. We may also turn it inward, and become ill, anxious and depressed.

The secret to keeping a balloon from blowing up is really quite simple. You stop putting air in, and you let some of the air out. To keep ourselves from blowing up is the same principle. We have to stop putting so much stress in our lives. We have to set our limits and realize our own limitations and respect them. Also, when we realize our balloon is too full, we need to let some air out. We do this by taking care of ourselves. We take some time out, take a walk, take a vacation. We reorganize our priorities and belongings. We learn to say "no" to others' demands on our time and life. We do whatever we need to do to decompress and relax, simply because our sobriety demands it of us.

37. Sometimes You Just Gotta Follow the Doctor's Orders.

When we get sick or injured, many times we end up at the doctor's office. The doctor will perform his examination, and according to scientific procedures, make a diagnosis, and from there prescribe a treatment procedure. Aside from stitches, casts, and other medical procedures, the doctor will also sit us down and talk to us. She will tell us how to take care of our injury or illness. She may prescribe certain medications and give directions for taking them. She may also recommend a specialist, certain diets or exercise.

The rest is up to us. Once we leave the doctor's office we are on our own. Most of us would say it would be foolish to ignore the doctor's advise. The doctor, being the expert, knows how we should treat our problem, but she can't do it for us. We have to take responsibility and simply follow the doctor's orders. Sometimes, the directions don't make much sense, or it may include diets, medicines, or routines that we don't particularly like. Here's where faith in the doctor comes in. We know that the doctor is acting with our best interest in mind, and the doctor has training, knowledge and experience that we don't. So, we shut up and follow the doctor's orders.

The same applies to getting sober. When we first enter treatment or start attending meetings, we are told by treatment professionals or other recovering addicts to do certain things. Some of these might not make sense, or might even go against our grain. But if we can put some faith in those who have been where we have been, and have come out of it sober and free, then we have a prescription for getting better ourselves. All it takes is a little faith in those who know how to help us.

38. Medicine Wasn't Designed to Taste Good.

If you can remember taking medicine as a child, you will probably also remember grimacing at the taste of it. We all hated to take medicine as kids. Even though we knew it was good for us, and would eventually make us feel better, we hated the taste. Even the medicine that was supposed to taste good somehow didn't. Anyways, as much as we would complain and whine, our parents made us take it. They knew it was good for us even when we doubted. They could see further down the road than us, and knew that if we put the needs of our health before the needs of our taste-buds, we would be better off for it.

As recovering addicts, we often have to make the same choices. We are so used to dodging things that don't make us feel good. Feelings of guilt and shame, anger and resentment, and plain old general fear, are emotions we used to cover up, avoid, and get through with help from our chemical friends. Now that those friends are gone, we have to learn how to deal with these troubling emotions without them.

In order to learn how to deal with these emotions, and not let them well up and kill us, we sometimes have to do things that make us uncomfortable. We have to learn to make amends, ask forgiveness, admit our role in our arguments and wrongdoings, and learn to let go of perceived slights, insults, and abuses. These are not easy tasks, and when first faced with them we may balk and try to find a way around the things that we should do. There is however, no good way to avoid these things. The best we can do in these situations, when we are required to apologize, to surrender, to let go, to forgive, is to just do it, and swallow the medicine. It wasn't designed to taste good, or be a pleasant experience, but the long term results are certainly worth it, for by bucking up and taking our medicine, we continue to stay sober, and keep our humanity.

39. Being Open Is More Than Being Honest.

Many times in our life we have been asked to be honest. We have been told not to lie by our parents, our teachers, and others. We have learned this game well. As addicts, we have learned to bend the truth, stretch the truth, and generally lie through our teeth, and make the whole world believe just what we want them to believe. This is a great skill, necessary for used-car salesmen and politicians. For us however, it can do us little good. When we say that we practice a program of rigorous honesty, we mean that we are honest with ourselves and with others. Of course, as addicts, we know how to be completely honest and yet hide the whole truth. Did we drink last night? No, of course not, we will say, being completely honest. What we won't say is that perhaps we abused our pain medicine, or smoked pot.

That kind of honesty will do us no good. Of course we are honest with those who are trying to help us, but by withholding the absolute truth, and being completely open, we will consign ourselves right back to relapse. The honesty we need when we are trying to get sober is one that the Big Book of AA calls "rigorous honesty". This is an openness that reveals anything and everything that may be harmful to our sobriety, whether we feel comfortable revealing it or not. We go against our addictive mind-set and just like children, we put our trust in those who are trying to help us. For us addicts, confession is not only good for the soul, it's also good for our sobriety.

40. Being Sober Takes Practice.

When we first get sober, sometimes we get on what is called a "pink cloud". Everything is rosy and fine, our future looks bright, and we feel we may have easily licked the drug problem. We don't have the cravings, and are able to resist the temptations that others seem to have problems with. We are on a natural high. "That wasn't so bad," we may tell ourselves. "It was easier than I thought it would be."

However, it isn't long before reality rears its ugly head. Stress, anger, fear, loneliness, and boredom begins to set in. We want relief from our situation, our emotions, and want to be around those we are familiar with. We might even tell ourselves that we can handle a beer or two, or perhaps if we stay away from the hard stuff, we will be OK, or even perhaps we can hang around our old using buddies and remain sober.

Addiction is called "cunning, baffling, and powerful" for a reason. Our addiction can sneak up on us when we least expect it, and seem innocent and harmless. It isn't long though, before we are right back where we started from, or worse, realizing that we had promised ourselves that this wouldn't happen again.

When we relapse, there are two things we can do. One is we can ignore our previous attempts at sobriety and continue to use. The second, and of course the hardest, is to do whatever is necessary to get ourselves sober again. Slips happen, as does full blown relapses. These can kill us, but they don't have to. We didn't learn to walk perfectly the first time we stood up. We had to fall down a few times, and we learned from each of them. Now that we are learning to stay sober, it may take some practice before we get it right, but as long as we keep getting back up each time we fall, we will continue to get better.

CPSIA information can be obtained at www.ICGtesting.com
Printed in the USA
BVOW06s1449041013

332805BV00003B/942/P